The Senses

TASTE

Angela Royston

Chrysalis Children's Books

First published in the UK in 2005 by
Chrysalis Children's Books
An imprint of Chrysalis Books Group Plc,
The Chrysalis Building, Bramley Road,
London W10 6SP

ISBN 1 84458 166 7

British Library Cataloguing in Publication Data
for this book is available from the British Library.

Editorial Manager *Joyce Bentley*
Senior Editor *Rasha Elsaeed*
Editorial Assistant *Camilla Lloyd*

Produced by Bender Richardson White
Project Editor *Lionel Bender*
Designer *Ben White*
Production *Kim Richardson*
Picture Researcher *Cathy Stastny*
Cover Make-up *Mike Pilley, Radius*

Printed in China

10 9 8 7 6 5 4 3 2 1

Words in **bold** can be found in New words on page 31.

Typography *Natascha Frensch*
Read Regular, READ SMALLCAPS and Read Space; European Community Design Registration 2003
and Copyright © Natascha Frensch 2001-2004 Read Medium, **Read Black** and *Read Slanted*
Copyright © Natascha Frensch 2003-2004

READ™ is a revolutionary new typeface that will enchance children's understanding through clear, easily
recognisable character shapes. With its evenly spaced and carefully designed characters, READ™ will help
children at all stages to improve their literacy skills, and is ideal for young readers, reluctant readers and
especially children with dyslexia.

Picture credits

Cover: Bubbles/Angela Knapp. Inside: Bubbles: pages 1 (Jennie Woodcock), 4 (Loisjoy Thurstun), 5 (Sarah Vivian Prescot), 8 (Pauline
Cutler), 9 (Loisjoy Thurstun), 13 (Loisjoy Thurstun), 17 (Claire Paxton), 18 (Loisjoy Thurstun), 19 (Loisjoy Thurstun), 21 (Lucy Tizard), 22
(Jennie Woodcock), 25 (Lucy Tizard), 26 (Angela Hampton), 27 (Lucy Tizard), 28 (Loisjoy Thurstun), 29 (David Robinson). Corbis Images
Inc: page 24 (Lois Ellen Frank). Educationphotos.co.uk/Walmsley: pages 10, 14. Steve Gorton: pages 2, 6, 7, 11, 12, 15, 16, 20, 23.

Contents

What is taste?

Taste is the **sense** that tells you about the **flavours** of foods that you eat and liquids you drink.

Your tongue and brain work together to give you a sense of taste.

In the mouth

Your tongue is wet and covered with lots of small bumps.

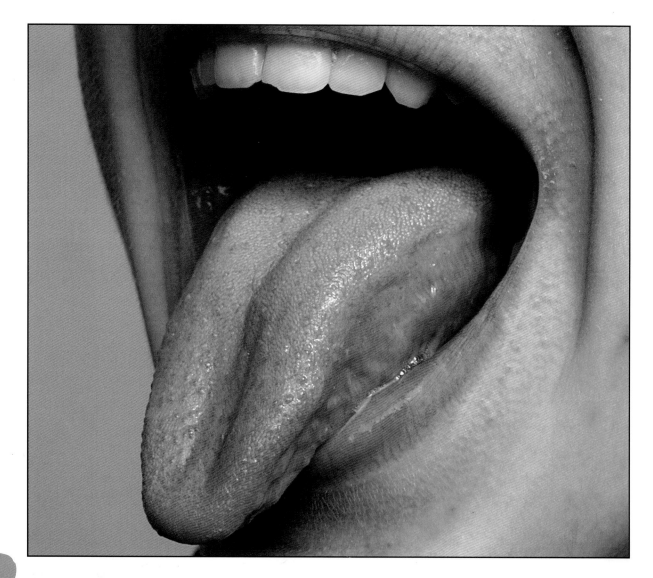

Inside the bumps are **nerve endings** that detect the different kinds of flavours.

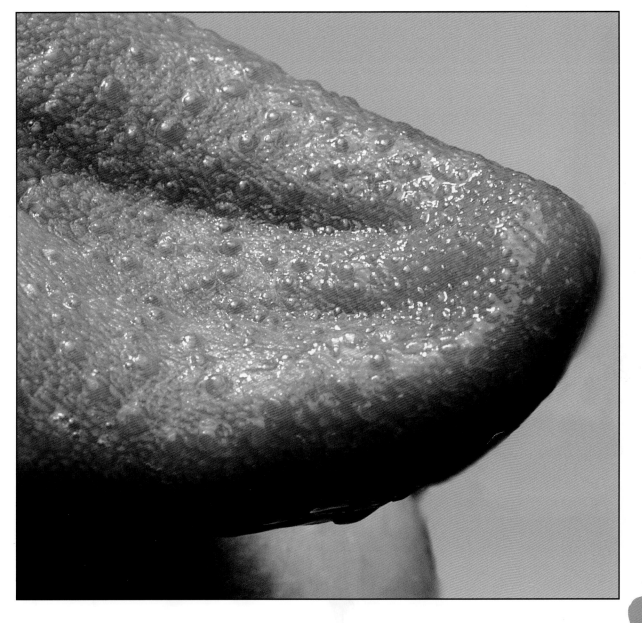

How you taste

When you eat or drink, some of the food or liquid goes into your **taste buds**.

The buds send flavour messages to your brain, which tells you the taste of food and drink.

Mixed flavours

You taste something by recognising its flavour. This can be salty, **sour**, **sweet** or bitter.

The taste of every food is a mix of some or all of these flavours.

Sweet tastes

Most people like things that taste sweet. Sweet foods are made mainly of sugar.

Cakes, biscuits, jams, honey, candies and toffees – which are your favourite sweet foods?

Salty tastes

Some people like salty food. They add salt to such foods as chips or boiled eggs.

Salt is added to snack foods, such as crisps and peanuts, to make them more tasty.

Sour tastes

Foods in vinegar taste very sour. Sour foods taste sharp or **acidic**.

Pickles and lemons taste sour. Fruits can be sour if they are not **ripe**.

Bitter tastes

Dark chocolate tastes bitter. Strong tea and coffee can taste bitter without milk or sugar.

Onion has a strong, bitter taste, too. Many people find bitter tastes unpleasant.

Spicy tastes

When foods are spicy or peppery, they are 'hot'. They have very strong flavours.

Do you like pizzas? These are often made with spicy peppers and sausages.

Creamy tastes

Milk has a mild, creamy flavour.
It is nice to drink cold.

Milk is used to make butter, cheese, yoghurt and ice cream.

Tasty dishes

Adding sauces to foods changes their taste. Tomato sauce gives spaghetti a rich, fruity flavour.

Tasty meals have foods with lots of different flavours. What is your favourite meal?

Tasteless

Water has almost no taste. It is not sweet, salty, sour or bitter.

When foods have very little flavour, it is hard to say what they taste of.

Losing your taste

Hot food often has little taste.
Let hot things cool before you
try them.

Your senses of taste and smell are linked. When you get a cold, food does not seem tasty.

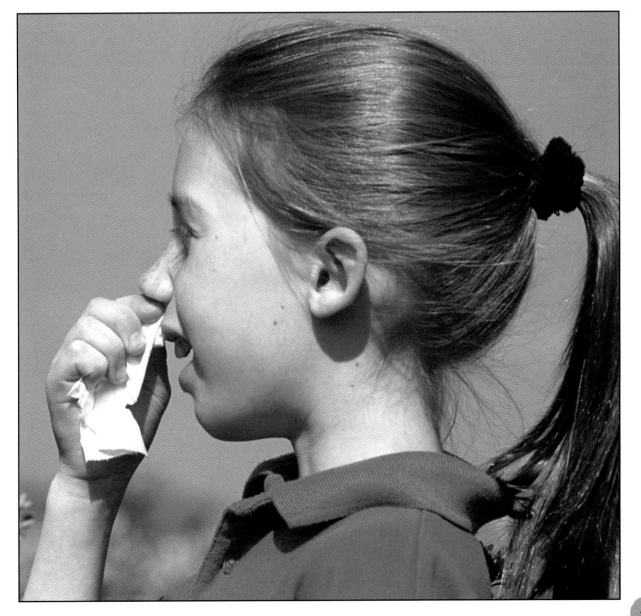

Quiz

1 What parts of your body are involved in taste?

2 What are the four main kinds of flavours?

3 What kind of taste is honey?

4 What is the main taste in crisps?

5 How does vinegar taste?

6 What tastes 'hot'?

7 What taste does water have?

8 What happens to your sense of taste when you get a cold?

The answers are all in this book!

New words

acidic tasting sharp and sour.

bitter not at all sweet.

flavours things in foods and drinks that gives each of them a particular taste. There are four main types of flavours – sweet, salty, bitter and sour.

nerve endings parts of the body that react to particular things, such as the flavour of foods.

ripe finished growing and ready to eat.

sense the way you find out about your surroundings. You have five senses – sight, hearing, smell, taste and touch.

sour very sharp tasting.

taste buds tiny parts of your tongue that detect flavours.

Index